MW00470988

Social Media Mastery: A Con
Growth

Rebekah Radice

Copyright ©2017 by Rebekah Radice

Published in the United States

About Rebekah Radice

Rebekah Radice, LLC (a division of RadiantLA) is a training and development company focused on helping business professionals use online marketing strategically. From email and list building to content and social media, our goal is to help you maximize, prioritize, and monetize your online efforts.

Rebekah Radice is a blogger, recognized social media leader, and the CMO for Post Planner.

As a speaker, she's been featured on CBS Los Angeles, ABC, and at the NATO International Summit. She's listed as a Top Ten Social Media and Content Marketer by Onalytica, and most recently, a Top Marketer of 2017 by Brand24.

Rebekah has been blogging since 2004 on one of the top social media blogs, rebekahradice.com - voted a "2016 and 2015 Top 10 Social Media Blog" by Social Media Examiner.

With her early days spent on morning radio, Rebekah has honed her skills at engaging and reaching an audience.

She is passionate about coaching, having trained thousands of business professionals on how to use social media, digital and Inbound marketing strategically, allowing them to maximize, prioritize, and monetize their online efforts.

In addition to being a popular social media and digital marketing specialist, Rebekah has also founded four companies. Each one leveraging social media for specific business growth.

Rebekah is dedicated to showing organizations how to use comprehensive online marketing to attract more customers, increase revenue, and position for growth through scalable systems and processes.

Connect with Rebekah and her team at www.rebekahradice.com

Intro

Intro

Have you ever wondered what separates those that are successfully using social media from those that struggle? Or why one business raises awareness, connects with customers, and drives traffic through social media while another staggers along?

If so, you're not alone! When I first started using social media back in 2004, I struggled with the same questions. I wanted to know how I could effectively use social media to market my business without a big brand budget.

But here's the good news, the answers and solutions aren't as complicated as you might think. Those that achieve exponential growth commit to daily activities, habits, and strategies.

While there's no one-size fits all solution, you can find the same success if you're armed with the right plan. Because a plan equals focus and focus is the fuel that will propel your business forward.

And as someone who works with marketers, small businesses and entrepreneurs daily, I know the power behind a strategy. I also know the importance of a plan that's engineered and then executed upon consistently.

It's one that allows you to act on purpose, flipping the scattershot marketing approach on its head.

Not sure where to begin? In this EBook, I'm sharing my own best practices. Each one is time-tested and will produce measurable growth when done right.

But more than that – they are each designed to boost your engagement, traffic and sales.

Here, you'll find the steps and tips to equip you with exactly what you need to take full advantage of all that social media has to offer.

By the time you're done with this book, you'll be able to use social media to market your business without getting bogged down by overwhelming details, terminology or daily to-do lists that keep you busy, but not productive.

Plus, you'll understand how, where, and what you need to do to build a successful social media presence. On top of that, you'll know how to identify the right social channels for your business, when to post, and how to create content that's appealing to your target audience.

So, let's get to it!

Chapter 1 How to Outshine the Competition

In an online world of "more of the same," creating differentiation is a must. While standing out can be tough, blending in is often the kiss of death to social media success.

But believe it or not, market differentiation isn't a new concept. In fact, in a Harvard Business Journal article from 1980, author Theodore Levitt stated,

"On television, we see product differentiation all the time, whether the subject of the commercial is a distinguishable good like an automobile or an indistinguishable good like laundry detergent. These are packaged products. How does the marketer differentiate a so-called commodity like isopropyl alcohol, strip steel, commercial bank services, or even legal counsel? They know that there is no such thing as a commodity."

Levitt goes on to explain why everyone has the power to win the customer from the competition and, having won her, keep her.

It's no different today. Whether you like it or not, assumptions are being made about your business. Your product, service, customer experience and online presence are all factors in driving consumer perception.

But it's so much more than that. Your personal brand also includes the reputation and relationships you've built over time. That's where Levitt and winning the battle over customer attention comes in.

Everything from your conversations, to your daily interactions define who you are. But more than that, social media is a very public forum where your treatment of customers, the words you say, and how you manage a difficult situation is all on display. While all conversations can't be positive, you do have more power than ever over perception.

The challenge for most companies is how to manage that perception and translate all that makes you uniquely YOU, into a brand that attracts, engages and inspires potential customers across social media.

Over the years, I've found that most fail at making social media work because they're focusing on all the wrong things. So whether you're just getting started, looking to reinvent your brand or accelerate your growth, let's first put an important foundational piece in place.

Before you can jump into social media and begin sharing what sets you apart, you need to identify your WIN (Who, Issues, Needs)

Here's what that might look like:

- Who are you speaking with on social media: small business, entrepreneurs, marketers
- What issues or problems do you solve: not enough time, bandwidth, budget, conversion
- What are their specific needs: create more content, social media engagement, ease of use, long-term solution, trusted system

Think about your WIN and write down 3 answers to each. Those will become a driving force behind your social media content and the positioning of your marketing message.

Unlocking your Core Strengths

Now that you've uncovered your WIN, let's talk about your core strengths. These are unique abilities, competencies, and skills. Have you identified yours? If so, are you leveraging them to the fullest?

I've worked with thousands of business owners and entrepreneurs around the world and one thing always emerges. Rather than focusing on improving strengths, they instead focus on fixing weaknesses.

Think about weaknesses in your own life and business. Do you see those as your Achilles heel, a hindrance to further growth? Do you beat yourself up over your them? I bet you do. It's human nature. But the reality is that focusing on your strengths is where opportunity for growth lies.

Consider this: would you benefit more from moving the needle on a weakness or a strength? And which one would you have more fun focusing on? The strengths of course.

Your job is to define that strength and leverage it to share your unique message and create differentiation. Begin to develop your personal brand by asking, and answering a few questions.

What are the top 3 things you love to do every day?

_____

_____

What challenge have you overcome that you're most proud of?

_____

_____

What's your biggest achievement and why does it matter to you?

_____

_____

Are you innovative or traditional in thinking?

_____

_____

How do you prefer to communicate?

_____

_____

What are the top problems of a potential customer that you can solve?

_____

_____

Now take the following 2 steps:

1. Answer the reflection questions and add as much detail as you can to your initial answer.
2. Take your answers and condense them into a short bullet point list. For example, the top 3 things you love to do every day might look like this:

    a) Talk with customers
    b) Write blog posts
    c) Design social media graphics

This activity should take you around 15 minutes to complete. And if you're wondering how they'll play into your social media strategy, don't worry! You'll see how we weave your answers into each chapter.

Chapter 2 Define Your Key Objectives

If you don't know what you want out of social media, it's fair to say you shouldn't be using it. Because there's nothing worse than a haphazard strategy with no destination in mind.

So, first thing first. Determine what you want to achieve.

For example:

- Build brand awareness
- Familiarize people with your product
- Attract new customers
- Improve customer service
- Engage previous customers
- Establish new relationships

As CMO of a bootstrapped SaaS startup, we're always looking for better (e.g. economical) ways to connect with our audience.

So for Post Planner, we might use social media to help people:

- Find great content without wasting a ton of time.
- Grow a following through predictive content.
- Get more interaction and engagement on the content shared.

Want to identify your own objectives and the key results you're going to achieve?

Start by writing down your big, bold objectives.

What are the goals, that when achieved, will completely blow your mind?

Begin with three. Then add the 2-3 key results that will come out of your efforts.

Here's what that might look like:

Objective and Key Result Example

Objective: Increase Social Media Content Quality

Key Results:

- 100% of posts optimized for social and aligned with company core values
- Improve campaign efficiency and audit process of all marketing assets with a >2% improvement in conversion rate

Objective: Increase Social Media Engagement on all Platforms

Key Results:

- Increase social media conversation rate by >25%
- Increase total reach of average social profile by >100%
- Increase total engagement of average social profile by >100%

Objective: Improve Brand Awareness

Key Results:

- Achieve 25,000 mentions on Facebook, Twitter and LinkedIn from social interactions
- Achieve 15 mentions in Blogs on Top 50 Social Media Sites

The key is to chunk this down. By starting small, you eliminate the feeling of overwhelm. Then you unpack each high-level goal into actionable steps.

Setting Your Goals

It's no secret that setting goals increases your likelihood of social media success. But, did you know that writing them down can actually make your social media goals stick?

It's true!

Statistics show that writing down your goals gives you a 50% edge over those who don't. But can the simple act of goal setting really be the key to succeeding at social media, no matter the industry, niche or situation? My answer is yes.

Clearly defining your goals allows for greater efficiency and effectiveness. Rather than posting aimlessly, you act on purpose. So, what else can social media goals do for your business?

They can help you:

- Visualize what you want to achieve with social media
- Make that visualization a reality through an actionable daily plan
- Map, track and assess your success, allowing for measurable results

While setting social media goals might sound simple, the reality is that most people don't take the time to put them in place.

If this sounds familiar, don't worry! Here's a few easy ways to make your goals stick.

Visualize Your Goals

Visualization is your first step and a vital component to your success. I will warn you that this isn't an easy place to start. However, dismissing this as trite or insignificant will set you up for failure.

Use a tool or app. If you want to establish new habits, put a reminder system in place. Lifetick helps you visualize, strategize and then track the status of your goals.

You begin by defining your values. From there, you set your goals.

This is one of my favorite features of Lifetick as it works off the idea that your goals should be SMART:

- **Specific:** Have you been specific in what you want to achieve?
- **Measurable:** How will you know if you've achieved your goal?
- **Achievable:** Is this a goal that you can achieve?
- **Relevant:** Is this goal aligned with your mission, vision and values?
- **Time Specific:** When do you want to achieve this goal by?

Write Down Your Objectives

With all the technology available today, sometimes my favorite tools are the simplest ones. Take a pen and paper and write down what you want to achieve.

How will social media support your marketing goals? What does success look like and how will you know when you've arrived? Be as clear as possible when writing out your goals.

For example:

Your goal is to create an enthusiastic base of company advocates. To do this, you must consistently share relevant content that your fans and followers want to read and share with their community.

You need to:

- Track and measure content shares
- Quickly respond to comments and questions
- Gauge the temperature of your community
- Analyze what's working and what's not

When you think through your social media goals in a linear fashion, you begin to see the full picture emerge. And for me, something magical happens when I see all of this written out.

The act of putting pen to paper allows me to mentally commit to those goals.

But I understand that this process isn't for everyone. If you'd rather not go old school, you can use a tool like Evernote.

Throw in One BIG Stretch Goal

There's no doubt about it, throwing in a stretch goal will feel scary. But don't worry, that's perfectly normal. Anything that moves you outside of your comfort zone is going to make you uneasy.

But think about this: what will happen when you accomplish this goal? Envision how you will feel crossing the finish line. That's the feeling that will propel you forward!

Examples of stretch goals:

- Attract 10 new business clients per month through LinkedIn
- Increase Facebook business page engagement by increasing comments to an average of 3 per post by (date)
- Increase blog subscriptions through social media channels by an additional 100 names by (date)

Chapter 3 Know Your Market

Have you ever read a social media post and felt like it was written just for you? That's what knowing your audience can do for your content. Once you've taken step one and know what they want, now it's time to write with your audience in mind.

Those two ingredients are the recipe for content gold!

Because once you understand their perspective, you can communicate in their language. Not many do this better than GoPro. They've perfected the art of User Generated Content combined with the simple, but targeted description.

If you want to stay relevant and viable in the mind of your audience, you can learn from brands like GoPro. The prospects and customers that you hope to engage with on social media are looking to you to solve their problems, needs, and struggles.

To gain a better understanding of what those are, take a look at your target market's interests, demographics, buying behavior, mobile footprint, where they engage on social media and what influences them.

Twitter is a great place to get started. Go to Twitter Analytics and then the Audience Insights. Here you'll find a wealth of information around your Twitter followers.

For example, what are their top interests? If it's Technology, you'll have a clear indication of what type of content they're looking to you for. As you can see, a clear understanding will help you better formulate and position the content you share.

Here are some questions to ask yourself as you get started.

1. List the benefits your product/service provides:

_____

_____

_____

_____

2. Make a list of people who have a need for the benefit your product provides:

_____

_____

_____

_____

3. Who are your competitors targeting? Who are their current customers?

_____

_____

_____

_____

4. Who do you want to reach:

Past clients?
Potential customers?
Industry experts?
Business peers?
Existing social media connections?

5. Have you identified your specific target market?

Yes ____ No ____

6. Who are they? (Explain in detail the traits and characteristics of your target market)

_____

_____

_____

_____

7. Where does your target market hang out online?

_____

8. What common characteristics and interests does your target market share?

_____

_____

_____

_____

9. Which social media channels do they use?

_____

_____

_____

_____

_____

_____

10. Where are they located and what's their time zone?

Location:

_____

Time Zone:

_____

11. Are they most active online in the morning, afternoon, or evening?

Morning?   _____

Afternoon?   _____

Evening?   _____

Once you've answered those questions, begin to build out your short mission statement.

This will guide you and your team as you develop your social media messaging.

Here's an easy formula to help get started.

FORMULA: *One thing you love to do every day + the person you help + your solution = your mission.*

For me, that would look like this:

One thing you love to do every day: Put a scalable business strategy in place

The person you help: growth-driven leaders

Your solution: create a comprehensive online marketing strategy to attract more customers and increase revenue.

My mission - and also the 30-second "elevator pitch" I can use on social media (or anywhere else for that matter) - now looks like this:

> *We are the first and only specialized consulting firm that helps growth-driven leaders connect online marketing with a scalable business strategy to drive measurable revenue growth.*

Take a moment to use that formula in your business and fill in the three blanks below.

One thing you love to do every day:

_____

The person you help:

_____

Your solution:

_____

Chapter 4 Choose the Right Social Networks

Ask yourself which social networks support your goals. Are they the same as when you started? More than likely, the answer is no. But that's not a problem. Most companies jump into social media without a plan or idea of how that channel will support long term growth.

But it's never too late to clean house. Take a look at which social networks are worth your time and which ones are wasting more time than you have to give. Here's an easy way to get to the bottom of that.

What social network(s) is your audience actively using?

Not you — your audience. This isn't about where you prefer to spend your time.

Research to see what social networks your audience is most active on.

How can you do this? Ask them!

Here are the steps you take to put this in motion. Remember, always keep it simple. This makes it actionable and easy to move on.

1. Create a poll in Google Forms.
2. Email the link to your database. Ask for their involvement and encourage it by offering a free gift. A Starbucks gift card can go a long way.
3. Post your poll on social media and ask for the same feedback.
4. If you manage LinkedIn or Facebook groups, ask the same question. You want as much response as you can get.

Now take that data and answer a few additional questions.

What platform(s) align with the type of content you share?

Not everyone consumes content in the same way. Likewise, not every platform is built to optimally allow your audience to consume your content.

Think about what type of content you share and pair that with your best social network.

- For video content – YouTube, Periscope, Facebook Live, Vimeo.
- For visuals – Instagram, Pinterest, Facebook.
- For business-focused content – Twitter, LinkedIn, Quora, Medium.

Granted, most of what I've listed above will work on any of those platforms. The key for you is knowing which one resonates the most with your audience.

What platform(s) are appropriate for your industry?

Not sure which platform is right for you? While there's no one-size-fits-all answer, there is a simple way to determine what's appropriate for your business.

Just take a look at your company and the product or service. How can you best position it to make connections and demonstrate the value?

For example:

If you're a health and fitness company, engaging your audience through video could be a powerful way to take them through your daily workout.

As a local bakery here in Los Angeles, La Brea knows sharing images of their latest creation speaks volumes to those looking for a tasty treat.

Are your goals and channels aligned with your target audience?

When you speak to everyone, you connect with no one. Don't cast a wider net for the sake of it. Instead, whittle down your options and align where you spend your time with company goals.

You also want to be specific in the what and who. What you're trying to achieve and who you're looking to connect with. The more you speak one to one, the better your message is received.

Chapter 5 Build Out a Captivating Profile

Social media profiles are how you present your story and message in a real and relatable way. They also speak directly to the search engines, so do your homework and know how potential clients are searching for you when online.

Not sure how to go about this? Let me walk you through a basic search using the intent of your audience.

Peg Fitzpatrick, social media strategist, does an excellent job utilizing every bit of the "about" space on each of her social media profiles. Want to rock your social media profiles and bio? I asked Peg for a few tips to get you started.

"Social media provides you with a ton of real estate for your profiles. Be creative and let people know who you are with some smart text, then add links to your blog and other places that you write, followed by links to all your other social media profiles."

Peg follows her own advice. Her bios are full of details that not only make her relatable, accessible, and authentic, but also tell a story to search engines and humans alike. A few additional ways to optimize your profile:

- Drop the pretense and have a little fun.

- Write your summary in an authentic way that allows people to understand what you do, what you have to offer and what you are passionate about.

- Conversations happen when you share interesting facts and tidbits that pull back the veil on who you truly are.

- A professional profile image – Your profile image should be considered a key element to your personal brand. For this reason, it is extremely important that you create consistency from one network to the next by using the same high-quality professional headshot.

- Use relevant keywords in a conversational and organic way. Understand what terms people are searching for when researching your business, niche, product, or service. Work those into your profile in a way that is conversational and easily scannable. Google is eager to help tell your story, so give them the ability to assist!

- Share details that answer the "what's in it for me question" and a link so the next step is effortless.

- Get local – As you craft your summary, remember to add your industry specific keywords as well as your location based keywords including city and state.

- Don't forget your call to action! Never leave the next step or follow-up action to chance. Do you want people to click-through to your website, your latest product or your book? Tell them!

Chapter 6 Define Your Look and Feel

Your look and feel is the visual definition of your online brand. From your website to your social networks, your online presence should express a consistent theme.

This includes your logo, website, blog, and any images shared on social media. In fact, images are an enormous opportunity to connect fans to your brand. Whether it's a picture promoting your latest blog post or a custom image around your most recent product, stay true to the look and feel that best represents your company.

Below is an intro to creating a brand style guide. Each section will lead you through a series of deeper conversations around answers you provided in previous chapters. Now pull all of that together to form your brand image.

1: KNOW YOUR PURPOSE

Use answers from previous chapters to fill in the blank below. The goal is to nail down the purpose of your style that supports your online brand.

My company purpose is: _____

_____

_____

Example:

- To express our vibrant personality and leadership to the marketplace.
- To consistently use our logos, brand name, and trademarks to communicate our brand message.
- To share the services we provide through integrity and authenticity.

Once you know your purpose, determining the remaining elements will become easier. You'll get a feel for who you are (serious and practical vs. funny and creative) and how your design plays a major role in relaying that to the world.

2: COLOR CONSISTENCY

Understand color psychology and the impact it makes on your audience. What emotion and feeling do you want to invoke?

- Black - power and authority.
- Yellow is seen as fun, joyous and optimistic.
- Orange is cheerful, inviting, encouraging, friendly and confident.
- Red is emotionally intense- we think of "strength, adventure, energy and love."
- Blue promotes a feeling of calm, and can symbolize loyalty.
- Green symbolizes balance, growth, freshness, and financial stability.

Choose a color that:

- Best represents your company personality
- The feelings you want to impart
- The action you want them to take

Start with your main color. There's 3 ways to find yours:

1. Use an online color picker. I like Colordot.
2. Upload your image to Imagecolorpicker.com
3. Download a Chrome or Firefox extension to find colors you like online. Give ColorZilla a try.

3: COMPOSE YOURSELF

Ever look at a graphic and gasp in horror? Or stumble upon one on a favorite Facebook Page that makes you oooo and ahhhh? That's composition! Similar elements draw the eye and create consistency in your brand.

Consider a square versus a star. These are two different elements. But when the square and star are both orange, they become similar.

The key is to create:

- Familiarity
- Consistency
- Flow
- Congruency

Think of your favorite band. When everything works together - the drummer, guitarist, keyboard player, backup singers, and lead vocals - what happens? Harmony! But when they're not working together? A tangled mess of chords and noise.

4: CHOOSE YOUR FONTS WISELY

Your font expresses your company personality and has a direct impact on conversions.

- Serif: Reference to the small lines that are attached to the main stroke
- Sans Serif: A letterform that doesn't have a serif attached.
- Script: Fluid letterforms that connect
- Display: A typeface that is quite decorative in style

Additional Style Guide Dos and Don'ts

- Don't use a corporate-style stock image (Fake vs. Authentic)
- Do ask "Is it relative to my topic and audience?"
- Do make sure the image has a bold focal point (share what a focal point is)
- Do choose images that are clear and easy to view
- Don't do the same thing as everyone else in your niche (contrast, color, hue, tone)
- Do ensure your images are relevant to your brand (relatable, new, interesting).
- Do make it obvious (just by viewing your images) which product or service you offer. What do YOU do?

Chapter 7 Create a Unique Experience

Take a moment and think about the last experience you had with a business or brand. What stands out in your mind and how did it make you feel? Creating a memorable experience allows customers to emotionally connect with your business. It's a personal connection that taps into the five senses we discussed above.

Why is this important? Because "people buy emotionally and then justify with logic." - Buck Rodgers, Vice President of IBM

While there is always a lot of talk about exceeding client expectations, creating a memorable experience is so much more than that. It requires that you have a deep understanding of who your clients are, how you can best serve them, and how you will provide what they need, when they need it.

Disney has always done an excellent job in connecting their brand story to avid followers. No matter where you look, you can connect based on childhood (or even adult) memories. How can you use this in your business?

Share Your Story

In our often chaotic and hectic online world, slowing down and taking the time to take people on your journey is critical. A great way to give potential customers a more intimate look into your business is to use video.

Share who you are, what you are all about it, and who you can help. Offer tips, advice, updates and relevant content in a short, easy to consume format.

Not only does Google love video (making it great for SEO purposes), but embedding YouTube videos on your website increases views and personalizes the user experience.

Here's a few ways to use it.

- Walk your clients through the benefits of your service or product. Turn your article into a video or pdf and then offer that download as an opt-in incentive on your website and market through your social channels.

- Take frequently asked questions and offer an instructional guide.
- Turn your product into a step-by-step instructional video. This allows clients to connect with you online in a very authentic way.
- Offer Weekly Tips or Tricks via video postcards. An online tool that I love is Animoto. It's easy to use, has built-in templates, and takes moments to put together a branded design.
- Share slides from a recent presentation on Slideshare and then turn that presentation into a blog post.
- Share thoughts, takeaways and your most important clips from conferences, seminars, and educational trainings through specialized boards on Pinterest.

Merge Offline with Online

While business seems to be more Internet-based than ever, you never want to neglect your offline efforts. Merging your offline and online is a perfect way to take an established reputation and introduce it to your new online audience.

Take your brochures, email marketing, flyers and direct mail campaigns and repurpose the content across your social media channels.

You can also take much of that content and turn it into blog posts. Did you answer a question or solve a problem in your latest email? Expand upon that and post it to your blog.

Don't forget to include links to your online profiles within your traditional marketing to cross-promote your online networks.

You want to make sure that no matter where your audience spends time, they can find you! Transitioning your established offline presence to an online powerhouse takes a bit of finesse. While this step may not feel like the sexiest of the bunch, it is imperative that you take the time to properly define your brand for your new online audience.

As Dharmesh Shah, Founder/CTO of HubSpot says,

"The goal of positioning is to create an immediate and direct connection in the minds of consumers; that's what branding is all about. Individuals need to think about positioning, too."

A personal brand that embodies your beliefs, expertise, unique abilities and personality will create differentiation in a sea of online noise.

Conveying that message effectively opens the door to attraction marketing and your ability to draw the right consumer to your product or business.

Invest in Your Brand

Whether it is time spent creating content or an investment into a new marketing tool, investing in your personal brand provides growth opportunities.

Spending money on the development of your brand can also build credibility, boost visibility and create a higher overall perceived value.

For example, spending money on your look and feel - a logo, custom website and branded social media channels - tells your story and sends a consistent message to potential clients. And you can do this even if you don't have a big budget.

The key to a powerful online presence is two-fold: provide valuable content and be interactive and engaged. In order to encourage the "know, like and trust" factor, always share your proprietary content in various ways. Here are a few ideas:

- Provide links, images, and posts that incite conversation and inspire action
- Ask irresistible questions people are dying to answer
- Share a video tip from your latest blog post and share across all of your social networks
- Draw on the emotions of your fans and followers
- Ask your fans and followers to share your content
- Include a powerful call-to-action such as: "Want to see more tips like this?"
- When promoting your latest blog post, don't just dump the link. Ask a question, share a story, or quote that draws your fans or followers in
- Encourage your followers to share their opinions and feedback
- Share other people's content, not just your own

Chapter 8 Design Your Content Strategy

It's no secret that content marketing is key to building trust with your customers. As Ron Guirguis points out in an Edelman Trust Survey:

"People don't just buy products anymore, they buy the companies that make products, the values they represent and what they stand for."

Sharing the right type of content will help:

- Prospects begin to recognize you as a the "go to" resource
- Build trust which translates into trust for your brand and product and makes you a top choice when they decide to invest in you or your competition
- Attracts visitors to your site, some of which may turn into leads, prospects, and buyers. If new visitors like your content, they will subscribe and share it with others. Both are key to growing a loyal following and a successful business

But you can't just share any content and expect to get great results. It needs to be the type of content that converts.

- Webinars
- Video tutorials
- EBooks
- Case studies
- Infographics
- Reports
- White papers
- Blog content
- Vlogs

In a world where your audience already has a massive number of hoops to jump through, you need to make your content easy to access.

Not only does content help build your brand, but it lets consumers connect with you.

90% of consumers find custom content useful, and 78% believe that organizations providing custom content are interested in building good relationships with them.

Here are three ways to design a great social media content strategy.

1. Curate Great Content

- Search BuzzSumo
- Look up keywords in Pinterest
- Look through "Featured" on Slideshare
- Use Post Planner's "Find" section

2. Get Visual

In a split second, your audience is making a decision. Will they stop and read or move on? Will they create conversation and engage your business or interact with your competition?

Given the speed content travels across social media, grabbing attention fast is critical.

Without it, you may lose an opportunity forever. That's where visual marketing comes in.

Great marketers know that visuals capture audience attention, increase engagement, and boost traffic. So where do you get started?

According to QuickSprout, there are 9 major forms of visual content you can integrate into your social content:

- Attention-grabbing, artistic photography – Think Instagram pictures or stock photos
- Creative video – Consider embedding sites such as YouTube, Wistia and Vimeo right into your posts or share them directly to your social media
- Screenshots – Useful if used right e.g. taking shots of helpful images of workflow or your products/services
- Infographics – Come in handy when you want to convey a meaty or super long message in an easy, bite-sized and informative manner
- Comics – Make a long story short, captivating and humorous with relevant cartoons or comic strips

- Data visualization – Present facts, figures and statistics in a simple and visually stimulating manner through standalone graphs and charts
- Memes – Use trendy memes tailored to fit the context of your updates or posts
- Miscellaneous graphics – Think of diverse images that complement your content
- Visual note taking – Think of casually designed layouts of ideas

Incorporate each one across Facebook, Twitter, Instagram, and more in unique and channel specific ways.

3. Don't Forget Video

There's no doubt about it. Video is hot, hot, hot. Creating several videos (produced and live) that support your social media strategy is a must. Here's where to begin:

- What niche or program can you spotlight? Whether it's you on screen or a screencast of your latest PowerPoint, connecting with your audience through video is imperative. A free program to create and share your screencast is Screenr. Just click "record now" and within seconds you are recording anything you can see on your screen. Then choose where you want to share your video instantly. Choose from Twitter, Facebook, LinkedIn, Instagram, and more!
- Record an interview with a vendor or local business partner that can speak to your readers concerns and offer tips and quick fixes. The amount of 60-90 second snippets you could create is endless!
- Create a video or go live to answer potential clients frequently asked questions.
- Discuss current events and explain how it impacts your client.
- Choose locations in your area and pass along fun facts and trivia. Pick a location and record a "Where's Waldo" video with one simple question: Where are you located? Make sure your location is easy to identify. Post this on Facebook and use it as a conversation starter or incorporate it into a giveaway.
- Record testimonials from your clients and post them to your blog and Facebook page as a way to boost credibility.

4. Create a Mix of Media

Your social media efforts require that you not only engage an already overstimulated society but increase your bottom line by providing fresh, relevant content.

To do this, add in a variety of content across various social networks. This will mix in with your visual, text, and video content we discussed above. Here are a few ideas to get your creative juices flowing.

Step-by-Step Guides:

- Walk your clients through your product or service. Turn your article into a pdf and then offer that download as an opt-in incentive on your website.
- Take frequently asked questions and offer an instructional guide.
- Turn your product into a step-by-step instructional. Not only do you allow clients to connect with you online and get a sense of who you are, but video is a great way to allow your potential clients to connect with you in a very authentic way.

How-To's and Tips

- Offer insight into your product or service and insight into what they can expect to gain by working with you or purchasing your product. What common issues do they face? What problems/challenges can you help solve?
- Offer weekly tips or tricks with a video tool like Movavi.
- Share slides from a recent presentation on Slideshare and then copy and paste into a blog post.
- Share thoughts, takeaways and your most important clips from conferences, seminars, educational trainings etc. through slideshows, screencasts and slideshares.

Blog & Social Media Content

- Discuss highlights and share insights from recent industry events you have attended. It's a great opportunity to give clients a behind the scenes look at your business and industry as you offer your feedback on what you learned or felt were the key takeaways.
- Create a marketing video for your blog post through Animoto.

- Create weekly webinars related to questions on your blog or Facebook page.
- Revive past content by re-posting videos, articles and trainings to Facebook, Twitter and Social Bookmarking sites.
- Ask via your social networks what the needs of your audience are and do this consistently. It's an easy way to stay topical and on target with the information your fans and followers are hungry for. Then take this information and write a blog Q&A that responds to their questions or concerns.
- Explain what a current event or topic means to your audience by either offering a unique perspective. You can also give details behind the who, what, why and how of a specific topic including the impact it will, or could have, on the industry.
- Take common myths and offer facts surrounding those often-misunderstood topics.
- Promote company news including changes, events, updates, promotions, new hires, etc. to allow the community to feel connected to the brand
- Survey your community through Survey Monkey about their most pressing questions and then use this material through an informational video or blog post. Share information in a way that solves a challenge, fulfills a need or offers support.
- Share pictures as often as possible. If there's an event or conference you attend, post the pictures to your social sites and write an article about it. You want your audience to become interested and engaged in who you are and gain an understanding into how you help.
- Ask hypothetical questions or tell a story to identify clients' needs.

Chapter 9 Create Your Daily Social Media Workflow

Now that you know what you're going to post, it's time to figure out the steps you'll take to increase engagement, traffic and sales.

This is your daily social media checklist. An easy to follow list of steps to take each day.

Your daily social media tasks shouldn't take you more than 30 minutes at the beginning and end of your day. If you don't have that kind of time, then plan on giving it away.

These tasks are critical to building your social media presence.

So, go ahead and create an easy checklist that will breakdown each step you'll take on a daily basis.

If you're looking to boost engagement, traffic, and sales, you'll need to put a plan in place - a daily social media checklist to follow.

Not only will it save you lots of time, but will make sure you're consistent in your social strategy and don't miss any crucial steps.

Here is your daily social media checklist:

Facebook

- Reply to all comments
- Thank anyone that's shared your content
- Like or Comment on a few relevant status updates or messages.
- Comment on five relevant Page posts
- Share relevant content to niche-specific groups
- If you're running Facebook ads, look at your stats and adjust accordingly
- Like a relevant business pages and start interacting

Twitter

- Monitor mentions via keywords and respond to any questions, needs, concerns

- Respond to influencers, make new connections and schedule posts to share
- Thank people retweeting your content
- Thank a few new followers
- Use keywords to find and engage with potential customers
- Go through contributors list, schedule retweets and interact with at least 5
- Schedule new blog post 3 times throughout the day with a unique CTA

LinkedIn

- Drop into other groups and see if you can volunteer answers
- Share relevant content in industry-specific groups
- Manage spam
- 'Like' three pieces of content daily
- Check to see who has viewed your profile (look for potential prospects)
- Thank/reply to those interacting with your content

Instagram

- Post 1-2 times per day – a mix of blog posts, roundup tips, top tips, funny/inspirational posts
- Share an Instagram story
- Like one post from everyone that's liked your content
- Search popular hashtags to find new people to follow
- Comment on other people's posts
- Send direct messages to new followers with a video and CTA

Pinterest

- Pin 5 images per day – a mix of your content and others
- Like 5 posts per day
- Repin 5 images per day
- Check notifications and thank anyone who's repinned
- Choose evergreen posts to repin to new boards
- Pin to group boards for added exposure
- Update boards or titles that need to be optimized

Chapter 10 Automate and GROW

One of the keys to successful social media marketing is smart automation. No, I'm not advocating that you become an auto-DM spammer or a content pushing zombie that never intends to engage.

What it does mean is allowing automation to support your strategy, keeping you on top of your updates while engaging with your customers.

Because we all know, engagement is the one metric that still matters. It's also the one area most marketers struggle with.

That's why it's important to incorporate a social media management system within your strategy. The right system and tools keep you engaged and interactive with your fans and followers and that equals social media growth.

Best Times to Post

Now I'm sure you've read one of those articles telling you the best time to post.

Know what the problem is with each one of them? They aren't you and don't run your social channels.

Each business (and social network) is unique. The only way to know your best time to post is to dig into your analytics. Armed with that information, you can make data-driven decisions. True Social Metrics is a tool I use daily to better understand when and how my audience is spending their time online.

Analyzing the data lets you see when your customers are interacting with you online. Rather than throwing posts out hoping for an outcome, you predict it with data. Once you know your best times to post, take those and add them to your favorite social media management tool.

For me, that's Post Planner and Sprout Social. In Post Planner, I can add those times to my unique Plan. Now here's where the automation comes in.

When I add content into my Plan, it's then scheduled based on those pre-determined times. It also sorts based on the type of content. No dragging and dropping or scheduling. Just add my favorite content and let the system do the heavy lifting. Pretty cool, right?

Sprout Social has a similar feature. Add your perfect times to post to your Queue and drop your content in. Remember, nobody knows your audience as well as you do. Do some research and get to know them – find out when they are most active.

And for goodness sake, stop getting online at all hours of the night to post content. Your business (and your personal life) deserve more than you can give without automation.

Automate Your Evergreen Content

It's no secret that your audience misses most of what you post on social media. Cutting through the noise is harder than ever these days. To capture attention, you need an easy way to stay top of mind. That's where evergreen content comes in.

What's evergreen content? It's content that never gets outdated or stale. It provides value to your audience, no matter if you post it today or a year from now. And adding it into your automation plan keeps it fresh and in front of a whole new audience. This is exactly the type of content you want to recycle and repost. One tool that's particularly handy in reposting evergreen content is Tailwind.

If you're a fan of Pinterest and its magical traffic converting powers, Tailwind is for you. Pin your evergreen content – blog posts, quotes, guest articles – you name it. Let it show up in your boards and the group boards you belong to.

To be clear, this is not about pinning large amounts of unwanted or repetitive stuff (against Pinterest TOS). Don't be a spammer or "that" Pinterest user. It's about sharing your most valuable content with a unique audience eager to consume it.

Set up Automation Between Various Social Media Networks

Most social media automation tools only cover a handful of social networks. That makes cross-promoting a challenge. The good news is that you can use IFTTT (If This Then That) to set up consistent automation. How does this work?

Let's say for example, you want to tweet every Instagram pic as a native Twitter photo.

With IFTTT, it's as easy as creating a recipe. A recipe allows the system to take action. When something happens on one network, it triggers another action on another network.

To create a task in IFTTT, start with your recipe. It's a quick process that's a one-time setup. Or you can use other's pre-created recipes that you can find here.

Chapter 11 Track, Measure, Adjust

If you're serious about social media marketing, data backed decisions are no longer an option.

Yes, there's always room for experimentation. But if you want to move the needle in your business, you can't throw darts at a board.

Not taking advantage of data is like stumbling around in the dark. That's why your content decisions must get backed up by real data.

But let's think about this for a second. What kind of data are we talking about? Statistics? Analytics? Research? The answer is "all of the above."

Getting Started

If you're new to social media or haven't collected your own data, you can begin by looking in a few places.

1. Case Studies and Statistics

Look to general studies to see what the standard, best practices, and suggestions are for your industry.

For example, here's a few generalizations:

- The best times to post content on social media is 1–4 p.m. on Wednesday, Thursday, Friday, Saturday, and Sunday
- Tweets of 100 characters or less get a 17% higher engagement rate, while for Facebook, question posts between 100 to 119 characters get the most engagement
- Posts with relevant images get 94% more views than content without them, and posts with photos get 39% more interaction
- Emoticon use boosts the number of comments by 33%
- Question posts get 100% more comments

Are these stats helpful? Definitely! Should you take them at face value and follow them like gospel? No.

The team at Buffer did exactly that. A Track Maven study found that the most optimal time to post on Facebook was between 5 PM and 1 AM ET. The study went on to say that the worst time to post was early morning.

After testing this theory, Buffer found that evening was a great time to post, but so was early morning. The least effective posting time was mid-day.

As you get started, follow Buffer's lead. Keep these stats in mind, but use your own data to adapt them to fit your business and situation. Use common sense as well. If you have a great tweet, don't cut it short or add meaningless words because you want to reach the 100-character limit. Do your own testing.

Try different posting times – not only the recommended ones. Find the times that work for you and your specific audience. Dependent if your audience is national or international, your posting times will fluctuate.

2. Buyer Persona

Making the right social media decisions comes down to understanding your audience. That's why it's so important for a business to have a buyer persona.

A buyer persona is a representation of your company's ideal customer. It's based on real data, reflecting audience interests, needs, and behaviors.

A defined persona gives you intimate knowledge of what makes your customers tick. To learn more about your audience, all you need to do is ask. Here's how:

- In person interviews
- Hangouts, Skype interviews
- Exit surveys
- Ask questions on social media
- Reach out via email

Here are a few things to inquire about:

- Age
- Educational background
- Marital status, family
- Role in their job

- Responsibilities in the job
- Interests

There's a lot of data to collect in order to get a full picture of your customer. Some information you can get by asking direct questions, while for others - you have to infer.

Here is the information that can help you better understand the buyer:

- Behavioral drivers – the how and why the customer has chosen your brand
- Customer's mindset – What do your customers expect from you? What do they love?
- Obstacles – what keep the customers from investing in your product or service

Understanding these can help you get a picture of who your customer is and what kind of content they like and need. Have that knowledge and you're all set to create custom-made content that your audience will love, engage in, and share.

Keyword Research

Once you are ready to create content, there is some data that can help get your posts seen. Remember, if no one is looking for your content, no one will see it. That is why you need to collect data in the form of keyword research.

There are several types of keywords, but the ones that you should focus your efforts on are buyer-intent keywords, which are words and phrases that convert for your specific business.

Here are a few tactics that can help you compile an effective keyword list:

- Start by brainstorming what type of words people would use while searching for your product or service.
- Use suggested searches. Type your business-related keywords into the Google search and see what keyword combinations Google suggests. Just make sure to use the "Incognito" mode.
- Do a search for your main keywords and look at the titles that are at the top of the search results.
- Look at the wording of the Google ads. The ones at the top have the best click-through rates.

Use Keyword Research Tools

There are a variety of tools that can help you find and choose the best keywords for your business.

- HubSpot's Keyword App lets you see the monthly search volume for the keywords you are considering
- Übersuggest shows you list of suggested keyword combinations
- SEMrush runs competitive research to review keywords your competition is currently ranking for and sneak peek into their strategy
- Soolve gives you keyword ideas based on info from Google, Wikipedia, Yahoo, Bing, Answers.com, and Amazon
- Keyword.io uses Google Autocomplete to serve up a list of relevant keywords
- Google's Keyword Planner lets you measure the search volume of specific keywords

Keyword research will help you gather data on the words and word combinations people are actively searching. Then, you'll craft content and incorporate the right words and phrases. Use keyword data to get your posts seen.

Use Analytics

Data collection is an ongoing process. As you begin, it's important to choose the metrics that matter most to your business.

Here's a short guide to the metrics you should track and measure:

- Conversions show you whether your audience is taking the next step with your company. Are they visiting your site, buying your product, downloading your freebie?
- Engagement measures the number of interactions per post. (comments, shares, retweets, or +1s)
- Reach is a measurement of how large your audience is and how many people you're reaching. You can see the reach for a single post or the entire profile.
- Impressions shows how many people saw your post in their newsfeed.

- Visits measures the number of people visiting your website. It compares it to the number of unique visits from people who are first-time visitors.
- Audience growth rate is the rate at which your audience has recently grown. That's compared to the last week, month or year.
- Influence scores show what social rating your profile has earned. Klout score is the most well-known score.
- Referral traffic measures the amount of traffic generated or "referred" from one place to your website.
- Bounce rate measures how many people visit your website and leave after viewing only one page.

Most social networks have free analytics tools that measure most of these factors. But if you're looking to dig deeper, here's a few more tools to check out.

You can measure your conversations, interaction, engagement, and shares through tools like:

- Google Analytics
- Post Planner
- Buffer
- Stats for Twitter and Instagram
- Iconosquare
- Sprout Social

When was the last time you researched what's happening across each social network?

The beauty in social media is this. If you stay alert, there's always an opportunity to adjust your sails.

Chapter 12 Use the Right Tools

Value your time online? Of course you do! And getting your time back is more important than ever.

If you're on social media, you know that keeping up can be exhausting. The good news? Having the right social media tools can make your life easier.

Fortunately, there are dozens of cool tools, and most are aimed at earning time back in your day. I've listed many throughout this post, but below is a deeper dive into 21 of my favorite social media tools.

1. AgoraPulse

AgoraPulse is a social media management tool that can make your life infinitely easier. With integration into Facebook, Twitter and Instagram, AgoraPulse helps you create contests, monitor your results, and customize your reporting.

2. Buffer

Buffer is an oldie, but a goodie (everyone has heard of this tool by now). Since its inception, Buffer has been saving marketers oodles of time. Although many tools have followed in their footsteps, Buffer retains its popularity and remains a favorite among social media marketers worldwide.

At its core, Buffer is a publishing platform. With it, users can schedule content to publish across various social media platforms. Thanks to Buffer, marketers no longer need to login several times a day to post content – instead you can simply create a posting schedule for each social network and queue posts to be shared at an optimal time. This becomes super powerful when you pair it with Followerwonk.

With Buffer, you can choose what posts to share and when to do it. And the best thing about it? It gives you back your time! Create a schedule for weeks and even months ahead, posting your evergreen content without lifting a finger.

Plus, their built-in analytics help you see what is working and what is not so you can quickly (and easily) adjust your course of action.

3. Buzzsumo

Great content is key to great social media marketing, and Buzzsumo is just the tool for that. It helps you find the most popular content and stay updated on what's happening in your industry. It can be used as a source of fantastic content.

Simply type in a keyword or phrase and look for popular content that's already performed well or type in the domain name of your competition and look at the most popular content they've shared.

Buzzsumo searches through different types of content including infographics, blog articles, and videos, and shows you the popularity of each piece of content in each social media network. It's a daily go-to tool for me as I'm researching a specific topic or looking for additional content to link to from a blog post like this one.

Any way you use it, it's a goldmine of insight into your target market's likes/dislikes. Use that info to better tailor your marketing strategy to the needs and tastes of your audience.

4. Commun.It

With Commun.it, you will never need to worry about missing a mention or important conversation again. Commun.it is an easy way to monitor your Twitter activity and respond in real time. You can also find and engage your top supporters to create reciprocal and meaningful relationships.

5. CoSchedule Headline Analyzer

Headlines can make or break a post, and that's why you want to make sure that yours is a winner.

Co-Schedule has created a headline analyzer that measures the effectiveness of your headline. In other words, how well will it perform? I use this tool daily to test out as many variations of a headline as I can come up with. Each one is scored based on their algorithm, giving me an idea of how my audience will respond to it.

6. Droplr

I couldn't live online without this handy tool. And if you work within the design space or manage a team, this will simplify your life tenfold.

With Droplr, you remove the friction and frustration of sharing files, shortened URLs, screen recordings and even gifs from your busy life.

7. Heyo

Want to easily create Facebook contests, sweepstakes and mobile- optimized landing pages? With Heyo you can! Heyo makes its simple to design beautiful and fully optimized pages that help you get more fans, leads and sales.

8. Inkybee

There is a reason why social media has the word "social" in it – it is all about communication and building relationships.

Any successful social media marketing strategy needs to involve relationships with successful influencers, content creators, and bloggers. They can link to your page, increase brand awareness, improve reach, and so much more.

However, in order to establish a relationship with this group and get them to share your stuff, you need to find and connect first. That's where Inkybee comes in! Inkybee is a tool that lets you look for top bloggers, websites, and influencers in a specific niche.

All you need to do is enter a phrase or keyword and the tool will show you relevant results. There are also ways to narrow down the search by applying criteria such as a specific domain, country, or social media engagement.

9. KingSumo

Because a great headline is that important, I've included two options. KingSumo is a WordPress plugin that tests out blog headlines against each other and then determines which one will attract more traffic. Pretty cool, right? It gets better!

KingSumo lets you test 2-10 headlines at the same time, which are then rotated and randomly shown to visitors. The tool monitors the impressions that each headline receives, displays it as a percentage and then shares the potential each has to perform.

10. Likeable Local

Likeable Local is a powerful social media platform that offers small businesses a simple solution for managing a social media presence.

As Neal Schaffer from Maximize Social Business says, "It's a scalable tool solution to small businesses who are looking for an easy-to-understand and easier-to-implement complete social media solution."

11. LikeAlyzer

Are you randomly posting to your Facebook Page with no clear strategy? Would you like to know what you can do to better optimize your Page? Look no further than LikeAlyzer!

With LikeAlyzer you get a comprehensive review along with tips to help you improve your interaction with current and potential fans and customers.

12. Mention

If you are looking for a tool that will help you monitor your brand's presence across social media and the web, then Mention is a real life (and time) saver. Mention, a real-time monitoring tool, detects any reference to your brand or keywords you're monitoring on all forums, social networks, blogs, and sites.

It also offers the option of responding to the mentions and sharing them making it a quick and easy engagement solution.

13. OverVideo

Video is hot, hot, hot. What better way to show off your product or display your latest feature than a video? Now take that video and amplify the message with an animated text overlay!

With OverVideo, you can take an average video and make it a real stand out.

14. Pocket

One of the most important tools in a marketer's tool belt is knowledge. But who has time to cull through the hundreds of thousands of articles written daily?

That's where Pocket comes in. Stay up-to-date on the latest trends and industry news by saving content to read later. I use the Chrome extension and the iPhone app to sync my content as I save on the go.

15. Post Planner

I can't talk about my favorite tools without mentioning Post Planner. Full disclosure, I'm the brand ambassador for Post Planner, but my love of the tool goes well beyond that. I've used Post Planner for years for a couple of reasons.

Not only is it one of the top tools for social media marketing, but one that can help you save time through proven content, creating predictable results. And who doesn't want that?

For those who are not familiar with Post Planner, it's an app that helps you manage and enhance your marketing strategy. In other words, it does all the heavy lifting so you can focus on what matters – building relationships, driving traffic and making sales.

But what really makes Post Planner stand out is that it also helps marketers find the perfect content to post. It gives you access to the most viral posts on Facebook and provides a huge list of status ideas. With Post Planner, it's incredibly easy to find content that is currently trending in your niche, so you never have to hunt for popular content to post.

The tool also provides a real-time analysis of the posts, helping you see what posts will help your engagement soar!

16. Quill Engage

There is no denying the importance of quality analytics. Unfortunately, not all analytics tools are able to provide data analysis that is clear, detailed, and easy to understand. Most are complicated with too many options and data that is difficult to filter through. That's where Quill Engage stands out.

This is a fantastic social media tool that connects to Google Analytics, scans it, and puts the data into a detailed report. It focuses on the most important information you need and reports any significant changes, whether good or bad.

17. Relay

Any social media marketer knows about the importance of visual marketing. It's also no secret that a significant portion of your visual content must be original if you expect to get great results.

But how can you create visually appealing content and do so over and over?

Relay is the answer. Relay is new to the scene, but quickly has become my go-to for creating attention-grabbing graphics in a matter of minutes. Relay has pre-designed templates with appropriate dimensions for an Instagram post, Facebook post or cover, presentation, and many more.

The layouts, fonts, sizes, and other factors Relay lets you choose from makes it possible to create professional looking content that will get noticed and shared.

18. Social Quant

Want to make better Twitter connections and increase your followers fast? With Social Quant, you can find relevant people to connect with that are interested in engaging with your brand. No more random acts of following. Get clear, get specific – get focused on your target market!

19. Sprout Social

Another superb, all-in-one, management tool is Sprout Social. I've used Sprout Social since their beta days and couldn't live without it.

The Sprout Social publishing system lets you schedule content on all of your accounts, whether it's Facebook, Twitter, Google+, or LinkedIn. It also lets you easily monitor any mentions across the major social networks and reply to them right away. There is even a mobile app available that makes messaging a piece of cake.

One of Sprout Social's coolest new features is their Instagram integration. More Instagram makes me happy!

20. Tailwind

My go-to tool for content scheduling and detailed Pinterest data is Tailwind. Want to make content curation, scheduling and analysis super easy? This is the tool for you!

21. Dashlane

Last but not least is Dashlane. With Dashlane, you can get your logins and passwords in order. Stop trying to keep track of your passwords, and instead let Dashlane do the work for you. And the beauty in this tool? You can get your passwords wherever and whenever you need them!

Chapter 13 Getting Started

If you want to push your business forward, you need to make sure it's valuable, relevant and accessible to consumers. You need to get — and stay — social.

Now that you're clear on why you're using social media and how you'll use it going forward, it's time to get strategic about your execution. Larry Wolff, CEO of Wolff Strategy Partners, a provider of interim executive and technology services says:

"95% of companies I consult with have strategic goals not met. This is due to a lack of goal setting and execution. A plan is either not communicated effectively to other team members or worse yet - no plan is in place - leaving the execution up in the air."

If you want to turn social media into the catalyst that drives you toward your goals, identify your purpose and then write with conviction. Always remember, social media success is only equal to your willingness to dive in and get a little dirty.

What do I mean by that? Don't be afraid to make mistakes. As Sam Rizvi, CIO of Post Planner, always says, "Done is better than perfect." Don't let your fear of doing something 50%, keep you 100% out of the game.

Keep pushing, keep moving, keep doing and most importantly - keep learning.

Get started today by envisioning the potential impact social media and an online strategy can have on your business. Now take deliberate steps to move your business forward one day to the next.

25766245R00030

Made in the USA
Columbia, SC
03 September 2018